Landscapes of the Heart

To ~~Nancy~~,

Blessings!

Cathy Cummings Chisholm
2/3/99

Landscapes of the Heart

CATHY CUMMINGS CHISHOLM

BRIDGE RESOURCES
LOUISVILLE, KENTUCKY

All photographs were taken by the author using a Nikon FE2 camera with a Nikkor 43-86 mm zoom lens and Kodak Tmax 400 black and white film. Film processing and printing was done commercially with the exception of "Urban Alley" and "Chorus Line of Trees," which were printed by the author.

Edited by Beth Basham
Book design by Pip Pullen
Cover design by Pip Pullen

First edition

Published by Bridge Resources
Louisville, Kentucky

Web site address: http://www.bridgeresources.org

PRINTED IN THE UNITED STATES OF AMERICA

98 99 00 01 02 03 04 05 06 07 — 10 9 8 7 6 5 4 3 2 1

Library of Congress Cataloging-in-Publication Data
Chisholm, Cathy Cummings, date.
       Landscapes of the heart / Cathy Cummings Chisolm. — 1st ed.
          p.   cm.
       ISBN 1-57895-063-5
        1. Devotional literature. 2. Photography—Religious aspects.
    3. Prayers. 4. Christian poetry, American.   I. Title.
    BV4832.2.C5287 1998
    242—dc21

                          98-33953

To the memory of my father, James E. Cummings,

and with gratitude for the constant love and encouragement

of my mother, Lucille, and the joys of my life—

my children: Wendy and Zach.

Introduction

I pray that the God of our Lord Jesus Christ . . . may give you a spirit of wisdom and revelation . . . so that, with the eyes of your heart enlightened, you may know what is the hope to which God has called you . . . .

—Eph. 1:17–18

T he real voyage of discovery consists not in seeking new landscapes but in having new eyes.

—Marcel Proust

T he tin was full. Not one more roll of exposed film could fit inside. For eight years, the container, which once held Christmas candy, had haunted the bottom shelf of my refrigerator. The holiday scene decorating the tin featured a snowman whose crooked grin seemed to mock my good intentions.

"Someday, I'll get into a darkroom again," was the promise I had made to myself in 1990. I had just completed an undergraduate class in black-and-white photography at Idaho State University and received my bachelor's degree in mass communications. The next step was to sell, give away, or store as much as I could and then pack up the rest of my possessions and drive across country with my two children to attend Louisville Presbyterian Theological Seminary.

I no longer had access to a darkroom, but I wasn't about to stop taking pictures. My passion for photography began in grade school when two of my friends gave me a Kodak Brownie camera for my tenth birthday. I've been taking pictures ever since, almost always traveling with at least one camera—and regretting it when I didn't— because wherever I go, I "see" photographs. Shooting a roll of film in itself nurtures my creative spirit. Black-and-white photography is especially satisfying.

Knowing that some professional photographers routinely store exposed film in a freezer for long periods before developing the negatives gave me the idea for using the Christmas tin to store my film in the refrigerator, just until I could develop it myself.

Months and years passed. I completed seminary and received a call to serve as solo pastor of a small church in a small town in rural Illinois. Two years later, a call to elected service at the denominational level added to my responsibilities and filled my schedule to overflowing. Every so often, another roll or two would be added to the tin. Every so often, I would promise myself that "someday" I would "do something" with my photography and with my writing, another lifelong practice and passion.

Until the fall of 1997, my life was full of transitions. My college-age son had left home earlier that year, and my daughter was married that summer. Traveling for church assignments, along with full-time pastoring, was taking its toll. Looming ahead was my fiftieth birthday and all the questions of mid-life self-assessment. What did the future hold? How did I want to live the second half of my life? Where was God leading me?

Then I discovered that the tin in the refrigerator was full. I just could not fit in one more roll. It was time to be realistic. I was not going to get into a darkroom again any time soon, maybe never. Although most of the film canisters were dated by month and year, I had only a vague idea what might be on the rolls. I selected five of the earliest to take to the local discount store for film processing. At least I would find out if the film was still good.

Two weeks later I picked up the prints at the camera counter, paid the cashier, and opened the first envelope. I pulled out the stack of prints and gasped. The first image I saw was a candid shot of my father and my son, taken in the last year of my father's life. I felt as if I were eavesdropping on a conversation that had taken place seven years earlier. The impact of that first photo continues to be significant.

A flood of memories washed through my mind as one image after another from places in the past came into view: camping along the Snake River in Idaho, a hot-air balloon festival in Teton Valley, the farmland of southern Indiana. Another five rolls, another two weeks of waiting . . . finally, the tin was empty. Hundreds of images! With each trip to pick up processed film, my excitement grew. And my consternation. Now I really *did* have to "do something" with my photographs—but what?

I shared the photos with family and friends. My mother and children were encouraging. "Combine your writing and your photography. You can do it! You need to do it."

A fellow pastor and spiritual director, who knew I'd had hit a dry spell in my life, invited me to take a prayer walk with her. As we talked and walked through woods and fields on a sunny October day, we tried to be especially attentive and mindful of God's presence. The result was a sense of peace and renewal—and another roll of film to be developed.

Conversations with a friend led to a suggestion that I try journaling as a response to the images. Journaling was already one of my practices, although I did not always do it regularly. Exploring the use of visual art in this very personal way for meditation and prayer seemed worth a try.

I began with a photograph of my son and daughter, taken during a painful time following our divorce. Words, phrases, feelings, images came to mind, and I jotted them down. The result was the beginning of a poem. More images, more meditating, more poetry. I played with the words and how they related to each other. A photo of paw prints in the snow led to my arranging the words of a poem down the page.

I spent the last day of December shooting roll after roll. Scenes of sharply contrasting brilliant sunlight and crisp shadows seemed to be everywhere as I looked across a snowy Wisconsin landscape. Of course! Being in the outdoors, feeling renewed by sky and trees and water, experiencing again the revitalizing excitement of creativity. I was doing something I loved to do! And it was something that gave me joy and nurtured my soul! Something I had neglected doing in the press of busyness. Like a thirsty traveler in the desert who comes across a pool of bubbling water, I immersed myself completely. Finally, I had to quit, not because I was too cold or out of film, but I was too saturated visually to continue.

Images lingering in my mind poured forth in spurts of handwritten words in a notebook. Sometimes the words tumbled out in the early morning as I was barely awake enough to reach for pen and paper. Sometimes I struggled to pull out even a phrase. I was beginning to find my focus, but I needed some feedback. Was I on the right track? Was this something that could be shared with others?

Knowing I would see several good friends and colleagues at a February conference of Christian educators, I began to transfer my handwritten notes to the computer. As I finished typing and editing the first poem, the words of a prayer flowed onto the screen. Again and again, a prayer was the response to both photograph and poem. I was reminded of the presence of God in everyday, ordinary ways. I began seeking the leading of the Spirit in a new way.

By the time I arrived at the conference, I had created a sample portfolio of my work. As I began sharing the results with close friends, the reactions were overwhelmingly positive. One friend used a few for her morning devotions. Another asked if she could use them for a women's spirituality retreat. The response usually included, "You have to get these published!"

One friend even approached an editor she knew and said, "You *have* to see what Cathy has done." A few minutes later, I happened to walk by her and we made an appointment to meet that afternoon. After the editor read the first few poems and prayers in the stack, she looked up at me and announced, "I want to be your editor."

Four months later, the manuscript was completed: a collection of fifty sets of photos, poems, and prayers. Over thirty different locations in ten states and one foreign country are represented. Wherever I happened to be, my camera was toted along, capturing what was before me—as long as I had the time and energy and light to take pictures.

I hope you find *Landscapes of the Heart* meaningful for your own life. I offer it to anyone who is seeking signs of divine activity in everyday life, in everyday places.

> May you follow God's guidance,
>   rejoice in God's presence,
>   and give thanks for the gift of "the eyes of your heart enlightened."

Acknowledgments

I especially give thanks to God for . . .

- friends Lucretia, Carol, Anne, Kris, Carole, Lynda, and Barbara, who listen to my struggles, offer immeasurable support and encouragement, and keep me in prayer;

- Sarah, who first told me I was a poet and who serves as my personal manuscript reader, and along with her husband Jim provides great advice and counsel;

- the congregation of First Presbyterian Church, Vandalia, Illinois, who have taught me to speak from the heart;

- the congregation of First Presbyterian Church, Idaho Falls, Idaho, who called me into ministry and loved me into new life;

- congregations in Tell City, Indiana; Terre Haute, Indiana; and Pleasant Hills, Pennsylvania, who nurtured me in faith and discipleship;

- Jane, Paula, Mike, and Tim of Idaho State University;

- faculty and staff of Louisville Presbyterian Theological Seminary;

- all my extended church family through whose prayers, friendship, and advice God has done marvelous things;

- Beth, Pip, Tony, and the team at Bridge Resources for their confidence and enthusiasm;

- the gift of the faithful and creative presence of the Spirit guiding my life and inspiring my work.

Landscapes
of the Heart

Birdseye-Bristow Exit
Perry County, Indiana
August 1997

The sinking sun
in the rearview mirror
caught my eye
and pulled me off the highway
    at the next exit.
There I found ordinary scenery
and a spectacular scene:
        Fields . . . Trees . . . Hills . . . Clouds . . .
        bathed in a summer day's last light.
An invitation to delight in the earth
and give thanks to the Creator.

Prayer

Creator God,
How grateful I am to witness again
  the beauty and majesty of your creation!
How foolish I feel for all the times I drive down the road
    in too much of a hurry to get somewhere else,
    too unseeing to savor the visual feasts you set before me.
No wonder my spirit shrivels from lack of nourishment.
Catch my eye. Demand my attention, persistent God.
Produce in me the discipline to be attentive always to signs of your activity.
Grant me the ability to distinguish between the things
    that truly demand my time and energy
    and those that can wait—
    or even be left undone—
While I revel in your presence.

Stone Steps
Natural Bridge State Park, Kentucky
August 1991

The trail demands I climb,
planting my feet on a rugged path.
Upward I am led
along a stairway of stone
shaped by the footsteps
of those who came before.
A solar spotlight
penetrates the wooded darkness.
Sunshine resting on stone
creates a sanctuary:
 Come to the Table!
In the midst of the journey,
struggling to put one foot in front of the other,
Light greets my eyes,
beckoning an invitation
  to rest
  to worship.

Prayer

Divine Light,
You break through the darkness of my soul
with spotlights of love drawing me to your path.
 Open my eyes to see your Way.
 Open my ears to hear your Word.
 Open my heart to receive your Grace.

Rooftop Patio, Presbyterian Center
Louisville, Kentucky
August 1997

*D*eployed as signs of life
in an airy urban landscape
Potted plants
Bask in the middle of concrete and steel
Hidden from view on a rooftop patio
Accessible by a door labeled:
Emergency Exit Only.

Prayer

*H*oly Joy,
What a treat to come across something green and growing
when all about me seems to be gray and stifling!
Thank you for signs of life in an unexpected place
   and the beauty of the earth high above the ground.
Thank you for gestures of friendship among strangers
   and the sounds of laughter in the midst of seriousness.
May my life be a witness to your joy.

Atrium, Presbyterian Center
Louisville, Kentucky
August 1997

*T*owering columns
hold up a lofty ceiling.
A wall of windows
look into the Center's core.
The exterior of two buildings
now an interior—
New walls and windows join together old
to create a cathedral of space,
A recycling of real estate:
    new times, new purposes
    new views, new visions.

Prayer

*T*ransforming Power,
You are such an expert at recycling,
    making the broken whole,
    redeeming the wayward,
    renewing the worn out.
All of humanity is your personal reclamation project—
recyclable material for new creations in Christ Jesus.
Give us new views and new visions
to discover new purposes for new times.

Rowboat at Dock, Southern Hills Lake
Clark County, Indiana
August 1993

A rowboat tied to a dock
has an empty look about it
as if it were forlorn at being left behind.
Waiting to be freed from its confining tether,
Bobbing in the wake of others' waves,
Anxious to skim the lake's surface
in the search of another day's catch.

Prayer

*F*isher of Folk,

Sometimes I'd rather be the one left behind at the dock.

But how can I refuse your call?

You summon me to step out of my past

    to follow you into an unknown future.

You ask me to walk away from contentment

    with my life as it is.

You ask me to sever ties that confine me

    to things that falsely promise security.

You compel me to lift up my eyes to see beyond my fears.

You invite me to follow your example:

    to trust wholeheartedly

    to give sacrificially

    to love unconditionally

    to serve selflessly.

You know the only way I can do all this is to know that I can't—

    not on my own, not without you.

Grant me the courage to answer your call wherever it may lead.

Mirror Image
Southern Hills Lake, Indiana
August 1993

Still life . . .
Still air . . .
Still waters
silvered by twilight
mirror lakeside scenery,
a Rorschach test of perception.
Reality and reflection
merge into a single image.

Prayer

Good Shepherd,
If only my life could so closely reflect your image.
But sin stirs deep beneath the surface of my soul,
the waters of my life run too rough to mirror your love.
Bring calm to my turmoil.
Bring peace to my anxicties.
Lead me beside the still waters of your Word
     to cleanse my heart
     to quench my thirst for your presence
     to restore my soul.

Chaille Farm
Jennings County, Indiana
August 1993

A lone utility pole
sets the scene in the twentieth century.
Little seems to have changed
from the time the farmhouse was built
long before Civil War divided nation and families.
An unpaved road still leads to a world
too practiced in hatred and violence—
While in this place,
Cattle and sheep still graze in pastures.
Chickens still lay eggs and roosters crow.
Fields are still plowed.
Gardens are still planted.
Crops are still harvested.
A family still works and lives with the land,
Following in the footsteps of their grandparents,
Knowing that their grandchilden won't.

Prayer

*G*od of the Ages,
Grant me the wisdom to know which ways from the past to preserve
and which trends of the future to guard against.
Help me to welcome those changes that are your will for my life.
Help your church welcome those changes that are your will for our future.

The Farm
Jennings County, Indiana
August 1993

*H*ow I hate closed doors!
How heavy my hand feels poised to knock!
How I dread the prospect of rejection!

"I am standing at the door, knocking . . ." (Rev. 3:20).

The childhood memory of a stained-glass Jesus
knocking at a heavy wooden door
reminds me that too often I am the one behind the door,
 that my heart is the one closed,
 that I am the one who does the rejecting.

Prayer

*G*od of Faithfulness,
I pretend not to hear your knocking.
My hand is frozen in mid-air, unable to reach out to you.
How I long to fling open the door to welcome you into my heart
that I can eagerly and faithfully
approach the doorways you set before me.

Farm Window
Jennings County, Indiana
August 1993

Remnants of farm life line up in the window.
Empty bottles testify to the work
   of preserving fruits of the earth.
Their simple shapes and earth colors
decor enough for a kitchen,
designed for the work of feeding.
Beyond
    grass
    tree
    field
Green with summer's growth
soaking up the heat of an August day.
Within
    the dark a cool sanctuary of remembrance
    of past times and lives.

Prayer

God of the Earth,
I give you thanks for the work of my ancestors:
for strong arms that guided plows down endless furrows
    and hefted bags of feed and fertilizer
    and carried pails of water
for sturdy legs that herded wandering flocks
    and tracked game through thickets
    and walked to school and church
for gentle hands which stroked and soothed
    newborn creatures and feverish children
for patient hands that kneaded and shaped and baked and canned and mended
and stoked and shucked and milked and churned and washed and scrubbed
    again and again and again
for faithful saints who trusted your guidance
    and gave thanks for your blessings.
I give you thanks for the legacy of my ancestors
who passed down the story of your faithfulness
by living lives of faithfulness.

Window on West Henry
Madison, Wisconsin
August 1996

$\mathcal{O}$f course we call them blinds!
They obscure our view,
Making us unseen and unseeing.
A filter of shade and shadow
separates
inside eyes from outside eyes.

$\mathcal{Prayer}$

$\mathcal{A}$ll-seeing God,
I can be so blind to my own blindness.
Trying to stay unseen,
I become unseeing—separated from
    sights of pain and suffering
    displays of joy and beauty.
When I crawl away into my cave of hiding,
Send your storm of stillness to call me out into the light.
Enable my heart to rejoin the world, believing and seeing.

Labor Day Flea Market
Vernon, Indiana
September 1990

*T*reasure seekers venture out
through leaf-canopied streets
lined by a jumble of booths
overflowing with wares.
A festival called flea market
spills onto sidewalks and lawns,
turning a country village
into a congested outdoor mall
teeming with shoppers on the prowl.

Prayer

*P*recious Lord,
What fun it is to be part of a festival!
    to be in the midst of strange sights and sounds
    to spend a day away from routine responsibilities
    to watch old friends glad to greet each other
    to see strangers share a common interest
    to observe a village energized by visitors.
How sad that I need to be reminded
    to be playful and fun-loving,
    to do that which brings joy.
Help me to enjoy the simple pleasures
    in the festival of life
    so that every day is a celebration.

Sparrow on Steps, Riverwalk
San Antonio, Texas
September 1997

A speck of a sparrow
pecks away
Picking up bits and pieces of food.
Crumbs crushed under the feet
of passing tourists
Birds going about the business of living
Ignored by humans going about the business of escaping.

Prayer

R edeemer and Sustainer,
You give life to all creatures,
watching over great and small.
Yet I so often take that life for granted,
as if it were something to be endured or escaped
rather than embraced and enjoyed.
Thank you for tiny birds and bright butterflies,
for blooming flowers and green leaves,
for all those things that say, "Life!"

Window, Riverwalk
San Antonio, Texas
September 1997

Closed
Clouded with frosted etchings
Sheltering vague shadows on the other side
Closed
Concealing
Protecting from penetrating light.

Glass, wood, brick,
Squares, lines, angles,
Softened by the slight curve of an arch
and a shaggy splash of leaves.

Standing in front of a closed and opaque window,
am I looking at it and unable to see through?
or hiding behind it and unable to be seen?

Prayer

Revealing Spirit,
You alone see into the hidden recesses of my heart.
You alone know my desire to remain hidden and unseen
denying your gifts
giving in to fears
shying away from challenges.
Open my eyes to see for myself
what you and others see in me.
Encourage me to embrace the opportunities you set before me.

Empty Chair
Christian County, Illinois
October 1997

Chair under a tree by a garden
   Waiting
     Arms open wide in welcome
An invitation to seek rest
from the whirlwind of human activity
To stop and sit a spell
    and be still
    and know . . . .

Chair under a tree by a garden
    Empty
An invitation to imagine
the chair filled with the presence of
Some One
    Waiting . . .
         . . . for me.

Prayer

Inviting God,
Thank you for pauses placed unexpectedly in my path,
   for moments of rest
   for times of stillness
   for plots of growth
   for ever-welcoming arms and
   the companionship of silence.
You set before me an empty chair of respite.
You invite me to your garden.
Help me to accept the invitation to be at peace.
Teach me that I need not wait so long or resist so stiffly
   the yearning to sit and rest
   in a chair under a tree by a garden.

Barnyard Buddha
Christian County, Illinois
October 1997

I didn't expect to find a Buddha
in the yard of an Illinois farmhouse.
Serene in contemplation
from his seat in the ivy
Silent witness to the daily demands
of a working farm:
     feeding   watering   mowing
      harvesting repairing   preserving
But then, I didn't expect my hosts
to be an aged widow and her daughter
Gracefully doing the work
they have done all their lives.

Prayer

*W*elcoming God,
Thank you for a day of prayer-walking
    in the sunshine and fall air
    joyfully seeking signs of your presence.
I give thanks for the work
    of those who tend the fields and gardens.
May their labors be rewarded with abundant life.
I give thanks for the experience of gracious hospitality.
May we all learn to welcome visitors
    as if we were entertaining angels:
the act of hospitality, a confirmation of your presence in our lives.

Fallen Leaves, Louisville Presbyterian Theological Seminary
Louisville, Kentucky
October 1990

Fallen, dethroned . . .
Leaves pushed from lofty perches
by the dwindling light of late summer
their work of breathing and feeding done.

Fallen, finished . . .
Dancing across a driveway
in ever-changing patterns
choreographed by wind and feet.

Fallen, pausing . . .
before continuing the journey
of life and death and life again.

Prayer

Author of Life,
Guide my journey of faith through every season.
Help me to shed what is dead and useless in my life
so that new growth can begin.
When wintry hibernation grips my heart,
stir my spirit awake again
with a springlike blossoming of hope.
Give me patience to trust in these fallow times
as steps in the process of being shaped
into the person you have created me to be.

Window on North Sheridan
Chicago, Illinois
December 1994

Schefflera frames the window
Scanning blustery skies
Keeping watch
for those few rays of sunlight
that stray within reach of city windows
in the gloom of late winter afternoons.

Prayer

My Light and my Salvation,
Some days seem so dark and depressing
that just a glimpse of sunlight
breaking through the clouds
is enough to flood my heart with new hope.
Banish the burden of gloom.
Lift my eyes to see the Source of my help.
Keep me vigilant for signs of your love.

Snowy Rooftop
Chicago, Illinois
December 1994

*L*ooking down
on what should be up
is an odd point of view.
I feel as if I am spying
on places not meant to be seen.
The snow-shingled roof
is tattooed by a trail of tiny footprints,
proof that another intruder was there first.

Prayer

*H*eavenly Mystery,
Why do I wonder if this is the view you have of the world?
We so often pray as if you are stuck someplace up in the sky,
too high and far away to take notice of our tiny trails of tears.
Open my eyes to unfamiliar perspectives—
to see the world around me from fresh points of view
to recognize you as a right-here, right-now earthly Presence.

Pedestrian Bridge, West Wingra Drive
Madison, Wisconsin
December 1997

Shadow lines
crisscross
A tangle of angles
suspended over icy waters
Bridge and river
working at cross purposes.

Prayer

Spirit Divine,
So often I think getting to the other side of the river
is a problem I must solve on my own
with fancy designs and complicated construction.
Help me when the waters of discontent
flow through my life.
Walk beside me as I scan the riverbank
for a way through the turmoil of indecision.
Remind me of your promises that will overcome my fears.
Welcome me as I reach the other side,
even though I know you were the One who carried me
on the shoulders of your strength.

Frozen River, University of Wisconsin Arboretum
Madison, Wisconsin
December 1997

*U*nseen beneath the frozen surface,
beneath the ice, a flowing stream
Blanketed by snow
Decorated with shadows
Guarded by rock-lined banks
The surface defies definition.
The eye can only guess
how thick the ice
how deep the water.
The river remains a mystery
Held captive by the cold
until warmth comes again to melt its mask.

Prayer

*S*ource of all Life and Love,
You see past the paltry shell of my pretenses
into the depths of my frozen heart.
You know when the river of faith
running through my soul is shallow and sluggish.
You feel the icy grip of coldheartedness
building a barrier between us.
Shine the bright light of your love on my face.
Warm me through and through with your grace
so that my spirit will run swiftly and deeply
and directly to you.

Prairie Bridge, University of Wisconsin Arboretum
Madison, Wisconsin
December 1997

A ladder of shadows
stretches across the bridge
to prairie's edge.
Steps lead down to a walkway:
wooden planks plodding
through the snowy woods.
Dual-purpose structures
provide access to nature's outdoor gallery
while keeping feet from mud and grass,
restricting human travel
to predetermined paths.

Prayer

*C*reating Mystery,
How I long to strike off on my own
and avoid the well-traveled ways.
How I resist staying within the lines
and following the path set before me.
Teach me the disciplines I need to be truly free to serve you.
Enable me to break free of that which stifles my creative spirit.

Paw Prints, West Wingra Drive
Madison, Wisconsin
December 1997

What
critter
padded
through
the
snow
leaving
a
trail
of
footprints
on
a
river
frozen
in
its
tracks?

What
path
does
the creature
take
in the
seasons
when
the water
offers
no
resistance
to
the tentative
touch
of
its
paws?

Is it an adventure for a critter
to skate on the ice?

Prayer

Ever-present Companion,
You know the journeys we take
and those we are afraid to begin.
Guide my tentative steps when the path ahead
seems too slippery or too rickety
to support the weight of the burdens
I insist on lugging along.
Grant me the wisdom to know
when to proceed with caution
and when to plunge in with abandon.
Remind me that even when I feel I have lost my way,
you have never left my side.

Snowy Road, University of Wisconsin Arboretum
Madison, Wisconsin
December 1997

Tracks in the snow testify to a well-traveled road.
But I've never been this way before.
I don't know what lies ahead.
Whatever is just beyond the bend
remains sheltered from sight,
concealed by an archway of bare branches.
To continue down an unfamiliar path could be risky,
perhaps even foolish,
or, just maybe, a wonderful adventure.
But isn't this how we live each day?
The future always just around the curve—
a mystery to the present.

Prayer

Faithful Companion,
Surely you understand
our human hesitations and anxieties
as we look down the road unable to see into the future.
We don't know what tomorrow will bring,
yet we keep trying to plan and prepare and predict.
Remind me to enjoy this day and every day,
to do what you would have me do today,
to trust that you will guide me all along the way,
around the bend and beyond,
in the adventure of all life and all time.

Chorus Line, River Parkway
Idaho Falls, Idaho
January 1990

A chorus line of trees
dances through the park,
kicking a tangled rhythm of shadows
across the last traces of winter—
Rehearsal for a new season.

Prayer

Creator and Redeemer,
Just when I feel overwhelmed
    by the world's wintry coldheartedness
You send signs of renewal to come:
    the warmth of bright sunshine
    grassy patches emerging from snow cover.
I know that the bright yellow splash of daffodils
    cannot be far behind,
    their trumpet-shaped blossoms
    heralding the promise of spring.
My hope is revived.
I want to let loose with an avalanche of alleluias
    and skip my way out of darkness
    into the embrace of your warming light.
Refresh my spirit and renew my energy
So that I, too, can dance with the chorus of all creation
    and sing unceasing alleluias!

View from Copley Place
Boston, Massachusetts
February 1998

*R*ectangular rooftops
and car-lined streets
march out to the horizon
to collide with gray clouds
and a hint of sunshined sea.

What giant dumped out a box of blocks
and called it a city?

Prayer

*G*od of all peoples and places,
What a colorful palette you have used
to create your children!
What an assortment of architectures
inhabit our world!
I give thanks for opportunities
to discover such an amazing variety
of cultures, languages, and customs.
Grant me the wisdom to welcome
new experiences and different places
as times of learning.
May I always have the ability to marvel
at the many wonders of your world.

Mall
Boston, Massachusetts
February 1998

Cathedrals are supposed to be
sumptuous sanctuaries with lofty ceilings
to draw the eye upward as if to heaven
Compelling the heart to respond in awe
and wonder with worshipful adoration
    of the Holy One.
Today we build cathedrals
and call them malls
Creating spaces designed
to draw the shopper inward
to storehouses of marvelous things
waiting for purchase
A place to practice the religion of consumption
with credit cards and cash advances
Seeking salvation in stuff.

Prayer

Giver of all Good Gifts,
Free me from my attachment to things
    and the seduction of consumerism.
Banish my fears and insecurities
    that seek solace in acquisition.
Forgive me for placing my trust
    everywhere but in you.

Muddy Road
Rochester, Indiana
February 1998

*I*s this really the road
I'm supposed to take?
Can this possibly be the path
I'm supposed to follow?
I don't want to
      Slog through mud and dodge puddles
      Plod along rutted tracks deeper into a dismal woods.
Where could this possibly lead?
Couldn't it be dangerous?
After all,
      I'm surrounded by shadows.
      My shoes are muddy.
      My legs are tired.
      I must be afraid.
Is it enough simply to make the effort
      to keep my legs moving
      to keep my heart working
      to keep my eyes open—
      to trust?

Prayer

*Y*ou know I don't always want to go where you choose to send me.
You have heard my litany of justifications as I protest your calling.
Persistent and Patient Teacher,
continue to be patient and persistent with me.
Forgive my stubborn resistance to going places I think I don't want to go
and doing things I think I don't want to do.
Teach me to trust the sound of your voice,
calling me to follow you wherever you may lead me.
Guide my every step that I may never stray from your path.

Tree Trunks
Rochester, Indiana
February 1998

*T*ree trunks
    vertical lines of life
      sturdy columns
Each one a circular history of hidden growth
       told in the counting of rings
A story made known by its death.

Prayer

*G*od of Faithfulness,
Thank you
    for all those things in my life
      that are solid and sturdy and still
    for reminders of growth invisible to the eye
      in spite of my impatient blindness
    for the Story made known
      by a death on a tree.

Urban Landscape
Atlanta, Georgia
February 1995

Steel structures sprout up
across the urban landscape
like magic bean stalks
trying to reach the giant's heavenly castle.
A city grows up and out,
producing a bumper crop of cubicles.
A honeycomb of buildings
swarms with worker beings.
Here and there a sanctuary
offers sabbath rest
to those who know they need it.

Prayer

You would think, Bestower of Blessings,
we'd have learned the lessons of Babel—
that you cannot be found
> by building higher and higher
> or acquiring more and more
> or working harder and harder,
but by seeking you right where we are found.
In the midst of the busyness of business,
in the everydayness of routine chores,
You are here, offering sabbath rest and refreshment,
whatever the time or day or place.

Daffodils in Snow
Vandalia, Illinois
February 1998

February doesn't know how to act this year.
Deceivingly warm days
coaxed daffodils
into emerging early from their garden burial.
Didn't they know that winter
couldn't possibly be finished with us yet?
Now the too-eager buds have been seared by snowfall,
pounced on by plummeting temperatures.
Will they escape with this year's blossoms?

Prayer

*G*od of Grace,
Too many times I have been seared by life's storms,
plunged into pain, frozen by grief,
unable to see my way clear out of the depths.
But there you were in the darkness with me.
I knew you would not leave my side.
Because I was not alone,
because I was loved by the body of Christ,
I emerged from my burial plot of pain,
ready to blossom again.
Thank you for your love and faithfulness,
Thank you for your love and faithfulness made visible in the church.

Grain Elevators
Altamont, Illinois
March 1998

*R*ural high rises
house the harvest of surrounding acres.
Concrete cylinders encircle
last summer's crops.
Storage containers
protect commodities
until market conditions
bid their contents to emerge.

Prayer

*G*od of the Harvest,
How easy it is to keep trying to store up treasures on earth.
Accumulation is such a demanding way of life
requiring space and time and care of all that I acquire.
What freedom can come from living simply.
But I can't quite let go of my stuff, not yet, not all of it.
Encourage me to be a good steward of all that I have,
of all you have given me.
Free me from the desire to have more.
Open my eyes and my heart to those who have none.
May each day of my life be a storehouse
from which others can receive your love.

View of Park from Women's Building
Seoul, South Korea
April 1997

An oasis of azaleas
tucked between a busy street
 and towering buildings
Invites
Delights
Offers calm
 from urban frenzy
A fountain of color in a sea of grays
A visual massage for city-weary eyes.

Prayer

*G*od of Beauty,
I give you thanks
 for the joy of spring blossoms
 for the delight of discovery
 for plazas carved out of urban congestion.
Guide my feet
 to places that speak loudly of your presence.
Guide my nose
 to fragrances of nature no perfume can hope to duplicate.
Guide my tongue
 to tastes of your sumptuous feast in every food.
Guide my ears
 to sounds of birds and breezes singing your praises.
Guide my eyes
 to visions only your handiwork can produce.
Guide my heart
 to seek your presence
 in whatever place in the world I may be.

Lamppost, Korean Presbyterian Centennial Building Courtyard
Seoul, South Korea
April 1997

The lamppost stands at attention
in the early morning glare,
finished with another night's duty
While the sun elbows its way into view
to take its fill of the day.

The lamp waits
unused
unneeded
unnoticed
Until night again paints the sky with darkness.

Prayer

Forgive me,
Guiding Light,
for thinking I can find my way through the dark on my own,
for being seduced by the false claims
made by competing sources of illumination.
Keep my face turned toward you
and your steadfast beacon of love.

Barbed Wire, Demilitarized Zone (DMZ)
South Korea
May 1997

*T*he demilitarized zone seems anything but—
Fences topped with barbed wire
Guard posts filled with sentries
Barracks crowded with armies
Unseen devices strain to listen,
    scrutinizing the horizon,
        supersensitively alert for the first hint of intrusion.
Soldiers
    Uniforms
        Guns
            Patrols
            Tanks
                Warning signs of war's readiness
Suspicion
    Hostility
        Pain
            Grief
            Fear
                Tension . . . permeate the air.
Is peacekeeping just another high-stakes game played by nations
whose armies face each other across an invisible wall of mistrust?
How do you heal a nation scarred by so much barbed wire,
when so many decades of division continue to separate
parents and children, husbands and wives, neighbors and enemies?
We who think we live in the absence of war
are stunned by the close proximity of its presence.

Prayer

*G*od of Peace,
We humans seem to be so helpless at the prospect of war.
Guide our efforts to build peace as passionately as we have sought to build armies.
Bring comfort to those who are war's victims:
    I guess that would be all of us.

Alley
Idaho Falls, Idaho
April 1990

LANDSCAPES OF THE HEART

A sideways glance takes hurried stock
　　of the dreariness permeating the length of the alley.
Necessary accessories of modern civilization are on display
　　　for those who would venture down this artery of urban life—
　　　　yawning dumpsters awaiting the next deluge of garbage
　　　　utility poles and their burdens of impulse-producing wiring
　　　　pipes, meters, gauges measuring out precious commodities
　　　　back entrances and delivery doors barring the casual visitor.
An alley is an in-between street
　　designed to keep the unseemliness of services out of sight,
Allowing us to cling to false front views of life.

Prayer

God of Justice and Mercy,
Forgive me for averting my eyes from dumpsters
　　and failing to see that some of your children
　　　see food where I see garbage.
Forgive me for avoiding urban alleys
　　and failing to see that some of your children
　　　see shelter where I see danger.
Forgive me for turning away from those
　　who are hungry and homeless
　　and failing to see that you are present
　　in the pain and suffering of all your children.
May your justice break through my comfortable contentment.
May your mercy guide me beyond my selfish fears.

City Beach
Chicago, Illinois
April 1994

Who would want to go to the beach
when you have to bundle up to keep warm?
Why walk along the lakeshore
when everything in sight is so gray?
The park seems deserted for good reason.
Perhaps the very desolation of the day
draws a few city dwellers to water's edge,
to open space and fresh air
and, even here, to more concrete.

Prayer

Inviting Companion,
Even on the grayest of days
you do not desert me.
Even in the coldest of times
you do not leave me desolate.
Warm my heart with your energizing spirit.
Paint my life with all the colors of the rainbow.
Awaken my soul from its winterlike hibernation
to a springtime of renewed faith and hope.

Foggy Morning
Vandalia, Illinois
May 1994

og
    obscures
    confuses
    mystifies
    beautifies
Fog
    promises serenity
    threatens danger
    to those who would venture out and into
Fog
    softens the hard edges of the outside world
    to those who stay safely behind
    encased by walls of fear
    more imprisoning than stone and steel

Prayer

Revealing God, to whom nothing is hidden,
I long to see clearly the road ahead.
I ache to venture out into the serenity of a fog-softened landscape.
But I am afraid
    of dangers that might be lurking out of sight
    of not being able to find my way
    of not knowing what lies ahead.
Lift the clouds of confusion.
Burn away the paralyzing fears.
Lead me into the light of your way.

Bird's Nest
Vandalia, Illinois
May 1995

*E*very time I open the front door
she greets me with a sudden flurry
of fluttering wings,
protesting my intrusion
into her pregnant waiting.
I have interrupted her work
of coaxing life out of the passing of time . . .
while I go about my work of rushing here and there.

Prayer

*C*reator of all Life and all Time,
I praise you for all creatures great and small.
Forgive me when I try to hurry along the work of waiting.
Forgive me when I take the work of waiting too seriously.
Teach me when to wait as well as how
So that I know when to accept unwelcome distractions
        as periods of relief and release,
or even opportunities to redirect my energies
        from self-absorption.

Old State Cemetery
Vandalia, Illinois
September 1997

The old cemetery is a collective memory,
cradling community history
in its grassy plots.
Broken stones and weathered markers
Sure signs of advanced age,
as if the place for the dead is itself dying.
A warning sign greets would-be visitors:
 No Loitering
  Violators will be Prosecuted
Lingering in the past
is a punishable offense.

Prayer

God of our Ancestors,
We are a forgetful people.
You command us to tell the stories of your saving acts,
to remember the lives of those who responded to your call.
Yet we neglect our history,
our memories fail,
and then we must learn all over again
lessons we should have learned long ago.
Teach us again and again,
that just as you were there in the past to guide our ancestors,
you will be with us now, to lead us into your future.

Wilford Area
Fremont County, Idaho
June 1994

Springtime warmth in distant mountains
harvests a winter crop of snowpack.
Cascades of frigid water
spill into streams—
a persistent descent.
The steady trek across prairie
is interrupted by a rock outcropping,
creating a surge of roaring foam
bubbling into the pool below,
Swirling in eddies before
resuming its seaward journey.

Prayer

Refreshing Spirit,
Let your energy fill my heart to overflowing.
Guide my journey through life's peaks and valleys.
Renew my strength when I encounter obstacles along the way.
Steady me when I panic in the midst of turmoil.
Spur me when I languish in the shallows of contentment.

Stand of Trees
Kelly Canyon Campground, Idaho
June 1990

Happy are those . . . [whose] delight is in the law of the LORD . . .
They are like trees
    planted by streams of water.

                                         —Psalm 1:1–3

A stand of trees
Trunks aligned
Gathered at the river
Planted beside an ever-flowing stream.

A gathering of trees
Trunks embraced by clouds of grass
Roots drinking deeply.

Prayer

River of Life,
Your Word is an ever-delighting river of nourishment.
What a joy to feast each day on the sweet taste of psalms!
Yet you know the temptations of work and worry,
which threaten to pull me away from the discipline of devotion.
Plant my life firmly in the rich soil of Scripture.
Root my faith deeply beside the still waters of your Word.

Banks of the Snake River
Madison County, Idaho
July 1990

*S*unlight dances with
swift water
darting between clouds
peeking between trees
to create a lingering display
of shadowy shapes at river's edge.
A tree leans precariously over the water
barely defying gravity
as if longing to plunge into the ever-flowing stream.

Prayer

*E*ver-present Friend,
How tempting danger can be
in its many disguises—
swift currents lurk beneath the lure of sun-touched waters
ready to disable the unsuspecting swimmer.
Nurture me in the ways of your wisdom, Holy One.
Help me unmask temptation's disguises
so that I may follow your path and do your will.

Tractor in the Field
Fremont County, Idaho
June 1994

Row   after   row
    after   row   after
    row   after   row . . .

    Up   and   down
    and   up   and
    down   and   up . . .

A tractor follows furrows
    Endless
    Tedious
    Monotonous
    Vital
    Work:
        Feeding the world

Prayer

God of all Work,
Thank you for workers who labor in all those ways
I don't.
May the work I do be an offering of thanksgiving
for the gift of each day of life.
May I use wisely and well
the abilities and opportunities
you have given me.

Irrigation Pipe
Fremont County, Idaho
June 1994

The irrigation skeleton
strides across the field,
the tail of its metal spine
disappearing over the horizon.
The monster is now at rest,
silent and still,
waiting to roar to life
with an infusion of water
pumping through its pipes,
ready to deliver a delicate mist
to the thirsty soil at its feet.

Prayer

Banisher of Fears,
So many monsters are out there
ready to roar new life into old fears,
and so many old fears
ready to create new monsters.
Anxieties feed on each other,
devouring my peace of mind.
Dry up the source of my fears.
Water the roots of my courage
so I can face both fears and monsters boldly.
Peace! Peace! Grant me the peace
that comes only from trusting in you.

House Falling Down
Madison County, Idaho
June 1994

𝓗ow much longer can you stand it?
 battered by gusts of wind racing across the prairie
 seared by summer sun's fiery tongues
 pelted by relentless rainstorms
 numbed by winter's icy coldheartedness
 isolated by walls of drifting snow
 worn down and out by years of neglect
 abandoned to the abuse of vandals.

What once was sturdy is now fragile.
What once sheltered life is now lifeless.
What once nurtured a future is wedded
 to desolation and despair,
 unable to shake loose from the death-grip
 of this place and its past
 to seek a new foundation.

Prayer

*G*od of Hope,
    what can we do
       to convince her that an unknown future
       will be better than the hell of the present?
God of Compassion,
    what can we do
       to convince her that your longing for her healing and wholeness
       means you are suffering with her?
God of Justice,
    what can we do
       to break the cycle of abuse and violence?
God of Love,
    what can we do
       to show your love
       when human love has failed?
Grant us the courage and wisdom
       to proclaim your hope, your compassion, your justice, your love
       to a hurting and hurtful world.

Steps, Mount Rushmore National Memorial
South Dakota
June 1991

*S*unlight
twists steel
into a zigzag shadow.
Strange shapes
careen down the stairway.
A crazy-making vision
confounds the eye.

Prayer

*G*od of Righteousness and Mercy,
So often what I think I see is not at all what is before my eyes.
Just as shadows play tricks with shapes,
so, too, do my prejudices distort your image in those
who do not share my culture or convictions.
Help me to recognize that you only are to judge.
Give sight to my eyes,
that I may recognize your image in every one of your children.

Windmill in Cornfield
Central Illinois
July 1991

*S*pinning metal blades
and sharp-edged leaves
whisper to each other
in the summer breeze.
Thirsty corn insistently
demands to be watered.
Windmills answer
to produce life-giving water,
propelled by the breath of life.

Prayer

*B*reath of Life,
Send your warm breezes through the fields of my heart.
Spin the motionless vanes of despair
with the winds of your Spirit
stirring up renewed hope.
Let the living waters flow through the roots of my faith
giving me a new season of growth.
Breathe on me, refreshing Spirit.
Fill me with your redeeming, renewing love.

Dawn Trinity, Teton Valley Hot-Air Balloon Festival
Driggs, Idaho
July 1990

A triangle of dawn sky
framed by balloons straining to escape their moorings.
Billowing envelopes of rainbow fabric
inflated by fiery blasts of early morning air.
Mountains formed by eons of cosmic forces
bulging into islands in an ancient sea—
A trinity of earth and air and light.

Prayer

My Light and my Salvation,
Must I see shadows
and feel your absence
in order to catch a glimpse
of the reality of your presence?

Mountain Sunrise
Teton County, Idaho
July 1990

*D*awn explodes
behind the mountain range,
Blasting through accumulated clouds
to proclaim its claim on the sky
for another day.

Prayer

*G*od of the Ages,
How many millions upon trillions of days
have you watched begin?
Could you ever tire of the thrill of a sunrise?
Could you ever be bored by the beauty of a sunset?
Forgive me, Creator, for taking your work for granted.
Let me savor the bold splashes of sunshine across the horizon.
Let me delight in the delicate brush strokes of shadows in the distance.
Let me soak up the scenery like a thirsty traveler in the desert.
Let me sing the praises of your artistry:

> *This is the day that the LORD has made;*
> *let us rejoice and be glad in it.*
> —*Psalm 118:24*

Ascension, Teton Valley Hot-Air Balloon Festival
Driggs, Idaho
July 1990

*S*lowly ascending,
the balloon hovers,
maneuvering to hitch a ride
on passing currents,
hoping to travel a route
unlimited by signs, signals, roads, traffic.
Envied by an audience of earthbound vehicles
clogging a pasture-made parking lot.

Prayer

*H*oly Wisdom,
my prayers ascend night and day.
I look all around for signs and signals from you—
Tell me!
Which way do I turn?
Which route do I take?
Free me from the limits of fear and confusion
to soar on the winds of your Spirit.

"Backside" of the Tetons
Teton Valley, Idaho
July 1990

*R*ain-darkened clouds
lumber over layers of hillsides.
The mountain range
strains to hold back
the morning sun.
A blanket of mist
clings to the valley floor.
    The other side of the mountain
      is not the view most tourists take time to see . . .

Prayer

Holy and Majestic is your name, O God,
your power to create and redeem amazing beyond comprehension.
Give sight to my eyes and understanding to my heart.
Let me see your world from new views.
Let me see the landscapes of my life from new perspectives.
Guide me through the mountains and valleys of the future,
that I may know your will and follow your way.

Paper Banners, Churchwide Gathering of Presbyterian Women
Ames, Iowa
July 1991

*p*aper transformed by scissors
coliseum transformed by paper
paper and coliseum,

    transformed by artist's vision into sanctuary
gathering
    transformed by worship into a congregation,

long banners of cut paper
suspended from rafters
girders and wires
a utilitarian backdrop of hardware
for such a display of elegance
and adoration!

Prayer

*C*reative Spirit,
Why should I doubt that you can shape and mold
the lump of clay that I am
into an earthen vessel suitable for carrying your love?
Why should I doubt that you can transform
what is ugly or evil
into that which is beautiful and good?
Shape me, melt me, mold me
through the touch of your artist's vision
and the energy of your Spirit
into the disciple you yearn for me to be.

Chalices, Churchwide Gathering of Presbyterian Women
Ames, Iowa
July 1991

Ho, everyone who thirsts,
    come to the waters;
and you that have no money,
    come, buy and eat!
Come, buy wine and milk
    without money and without price.
                  —Isaiah 55:1

The table is set
with extravagant abundance . . .
The invitation is issued
to all who are dry from thirsting
to all who are poor from spending
    on that which does not satisfy.
How many cups must be set before me
before I begin to glimpse the amazing gift
offered in a single sip?
How many loaves must be broken
before I begin to taste the healing peace
offered in a single crumb?

Prayer

Lord of Hosts,
Nurture me with the bread of life and the cup of salvation.
Be present at the table
    when I hunger for fellowship
    when I thirst for forgiveness.
Let the bread satisfy my emptiness
    filling me with your mercy.
Let the wine wash through my heart
    flooding my life with your love.

"Thunder Over Louisville"
Kentucky Derby Festival, Louisville, Kentucky
April 1991

*S*howers of shimmering sparks
—*boom!*
Loudly splash
—*boom! boom!*
an awesome array
of colors and shapes
on the canvas of a night sky.
—*boom!*
Missiles armed with bursts of beauty
blast heavenward
in a bombardment of thunder and light.
—*boom! boom!*
We spectators at this spectacle
Absorb the vibrations through the smoky air
—*boom!*
Collectively sighing
spontaneous ooohhs and aaahhs
Storing up treasured portions
of awe and wonder
to carry home in our hearts.
BOOM!
BOOM!
BOOOOOM!!!!!!

Prayer

*D*azzling Mystery,
You lift up my eyes
from an all-too-serious focus on life's struggles
to find delight in a display of fireworks.
Thank you for all your reminders
to live each day fully:
to embrace awe
to experience wonder
to celebrate beauty
to rejoice in the Lord—always.

Index of Photos

Georgia

Idaho

Illinois

Indiana

Reflections

Reflections

Reflections

Reflections

About the Author

Cathy is a Presbyterian pastor and educator who has a gift for serving on church boards and committees. In addition to photography, she loves to relax with a good mystery, do word puzzles, needlework, or take a long walk with family beagle, Casey.

Her love of landscapes began in the farmlands and wooded hills of southern Indiana, where she spent her childhood and was nurtured by family vacations throughout the eastern United States. During the thirteen years she lived in Idaho, she developed a passion for the skies and mountains of the West. One of her favorite words is *eclectic*, which explains her interest in sports, art, music, travel, and current events.